Wild Orca and Me

Ever since I can remember, my sister has taken me out to paddle.

She taught me how to hold the paddle,
and move it through the water.

She helped me stay steady,
even when the water and wind were strong.

She showed me how to read the currents and waves.
She also told me to listen to the sea
and that someday it might have a lesson for me.

Each day we went out on the water,
we saw something new and wonderful;

Eagles and otters,

seals and sea lions,

many different types of fish,

and boats of all shapes and sizes.
Some so big and so fast they created waves.

And sometimes, in rare moments when the world was quiet and the water like glass, I could see myself.

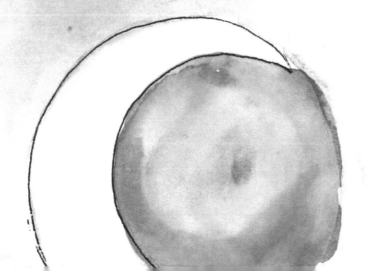

We have seen deer and bears walking along the shore.
They are not afraid of us because they know we are
peaceful on the water.

We have even seen humpback whales along the horizon.
But in all our years paddling these waters,
I have not seen my favorite creature of all.
The animal I have always dreamt of seeing, the orca.

*Until one morning,
when my sister
was tired and not
well enough to be
on the water.
I felt the sea call me
to go on my own.
And so I did.*

I carried my canoe over my head
and set it down gently in the water
without making a sound.

I paddled out in the delicate light.
Silently, I watched and listened.
I breathed in deeply,
making the only sound around.

The only sound until.... "pshhhhhhh."
A tall, dark fin sliced through the water.
An orca!

My heart pounded with excitement and then fear
when suddenly before the orca was within reach,
I felt a bump against the bottom of my canoe.

I was surrounded... by a whole pod of orcas!
They swirled and clicked and squealed and bumped
my little canoe.

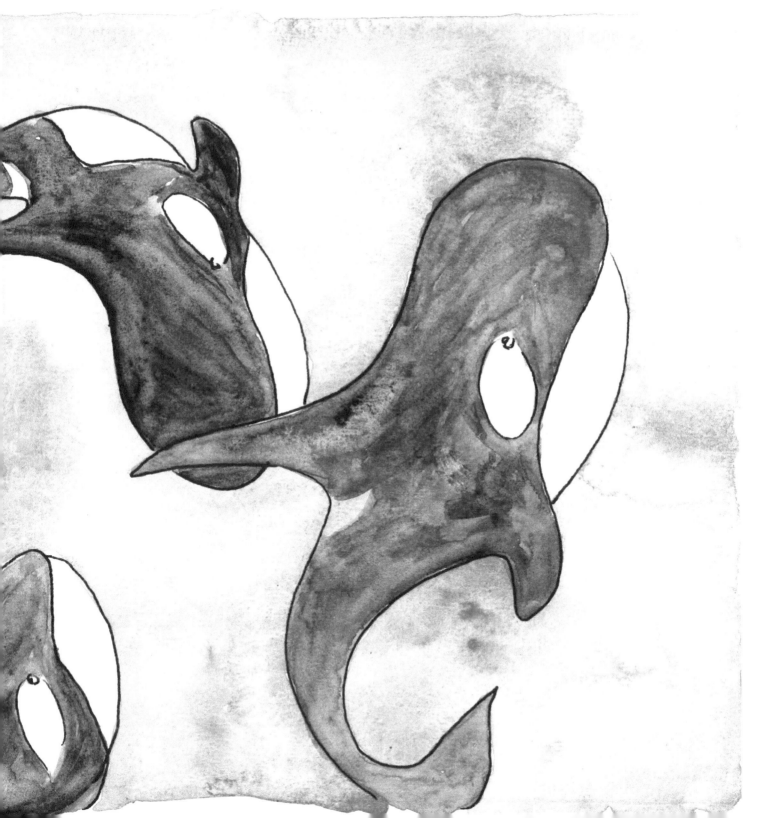

I took a few deep breaths, trying to remain calm.
The moment I had always dreamed of was happening,
but it was far more overwhelming
and scary than I had hoped.

And just like that, it was over.
The orcas moved on,
and I was alone.

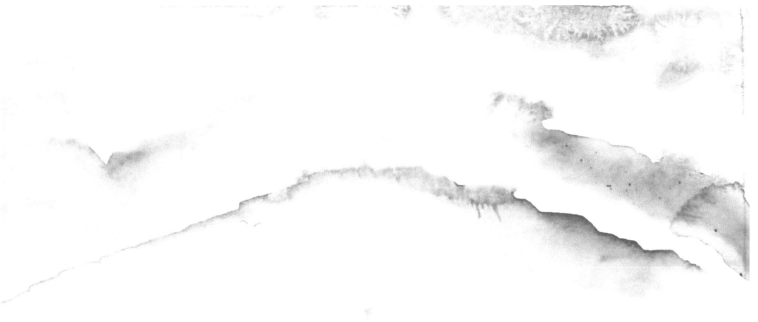

Even though the warmth of the sun was on my face,
the experience left me shaking and shivering.
I felt a few tears streaming down my cheeks.
I was worried that they would come back and
bump me out of my canoe.
I was only a tiny human,
not as strong as the mighty orca.

And as I caught my breath,
my heart no longer pounding in my ears,
the lesson hit me.
My heart.
My heart was alive and beating.

My breath pushes through my body and into the air,
just like the orca.
Because I am alive and wild, like them.
We are part of this world, and we belong.
Just like all of the other creatures around us, we exist together.
No matter how different we might seem.

And as I paddled back to shore,
I brought this lesson of the sea.
That we are all one and deserve to be free.
Free like the wild orca and you, and the wild orca and me.

About the Author

*Mary B. Truly grew up paddling and exploring the many streams
and rivers in Maryland that lead into the Chesapeake Bay.
She uses her skills as a painter and writer to express her love and
appreciation for the natural world we all share.
She hopes this story will help manifest her dream
of encountering a wild orca near her new home by the Salish Sea in
Port Angeles, Washington.*

CPSIA information can be obtained
at www.ICGtesting.com
Printed in the USA
BVHW022045040522
636052BV00002B/26